Introducing
Romans

Introducing
Romans

A Book for Today

CHRISTOPHER ASH

Series Editor: Adrian Reynolds

PTRESOURCES

Copyright © Christopher Ash 2013

ISBN 978-1-78191-233-1

First published in 2009 as the introduction to
Teaching Romans volume 1 (ISBN 978-1-84550-455-7) and
volume 2 (ISBN 978-1-84550-456-4)
Published as a stand-alone title
in 2013
by
Christian Focus Publications,
Geanies House, Fearn,
Ross-shire, IV20 1TW, Scotland.
with
Proclamation Trust Resources,
Willcox House, 140-148 Borough High Street,
London, SE1 1LB, England, Great Britain.
www.proctrust.org.uk

www.christianfocus.com

Cover design by Daniel van Straaten
Printed by Bell and Bain

MIX
Paper from
responsible sources
FSC® C007785

CONTENTS

Editor's Preface

Romans is one of the Bible's best known books. It is the book that God used to save Martin Luther as the young monk struggled to prove himself righteous before God. Reading and understanding it, he later wrote, 'I felt myself to be reborn and to have gone through open doors to his paradise.' It was a few centuries later that hearing Luther's introduction to Romans, John Wesley felt himself 'strangely warmed' adding, 'I felt I did trust in

Christ, Christ alone for salvation.' Many, many Christians have a similar testimony, and even those who come to the book of Romans as born-again believers find their faith sealed, built, steadied and developed by what they read.

Reading Romans will teach us about the gospel of Jesus Christ in all its amazing fullness and depth. However, even more, as you're about to see, reading, understanding and living the book of Romans will have a profound impact on both personal and church life. It's a good letter therefore for Christians to read on their own. But it's even better for Christians to read together, as churches (that was probably Paul's original intention).

This little volume is a brief introduction to the book, written by Christopher Ash, the Director of the Proclamation Trust Cornhill training course. Like all Proclamation Trust staff, he is also involved in a local church with his wife, Carolyn, in the centre of London.

Originally, these three chapters started life as part of Christopher's contribution to our *'Teaching...'* series. This series is written especially *for* Bible preachers and teachers *by* Bible preachers and teachers. They are more detailed than a devotional book, though not a full commentary; each volume is written to encourage those who have the serious responsibility of teaching God's Word in any context, especially through preaching. Each, therefore, contains analysis of what the passage means matched together with how it may be taught and applied.

In this edited excerpt, Christopher helps ordinary readers (that's all of us!) get to grips with the book. Firstly, he does that by giving us some important Bible background. In the first chapter you'll learn a little more about Rome and the situation there. In the second, Christopher guides us through some of the key themes of Romans, so you are helped to see what it is all about and what to look out for as you read the Bible text. In the third, we have included an edited version of chapter 1 of Christopher's longer book - it is based on the first seventeen verses of Romans and serves as an excellent introduction as well as showing how some of the main themes and ideas will develop.

I have edited these three chapters to provide you with a general introduction to the book. Like a traveller who steps off a plane or train at an unfamiliar destination and needs a moment to gather his or her bearings, this short book is designed to help you get your bearings in the book of Romans.

As you read, I sincerely hope and pray that your enthusiasm for Romans will be kindled and that you will come to see that

Romans is not just a collection of well-known verses. It is a rich feast, showing how the glorious gospel of faith impacts every area of Christian life and church life.

Perhaps you have been given this little book as part of a Bible study series or preaching series at church? Then, I hope it both introduces Romans well and gives you enthusiasm for what lies ahead. Perhaps you have simply picked it up and thought, 'Yes, I'd like to know a bit more about Romans'. I trust your prayer will be answered. If you enjoy it, as I trust you will, why not buy the two full volumes, *Teaching Romans* (chs. 1–8 and chs. 9–16), particularly if you are in any kind of Bible teaching ministry in the church.

About The Proclamation Trust

The Proclamation Trust is a U.K. based charity that serves churches by championing the cause of expository Bible preaching and teaching. Our aim is to equip and encourage faithful Bible preachers and teachers wherever they may be found, but particularly in the U.K. We do that through our training course (The Cornhill Training Course) and through conferences, online resources and books. Our *Teaching...* series is a key part of that work and there are currently twelve volumes in the series.

Our conviction is that where the Bible is faithfully and prayerfully taught God's voice is clearly heard. The call of every Bible teacher is therefore to cast himself fully upon God and, in the words of the Apostle Paul to young Pastor Timothy, to 'correctly handle the word of truth' (2 Tim. 2:15). Many resources, including our blog, The Proclaimer, are available from our website, www.proctrust.org.uk, where you can also read more about our work and ministry.

Adrian Reynolds
Series Editor, London, February 2013

STRUCTURE OF ROMANS

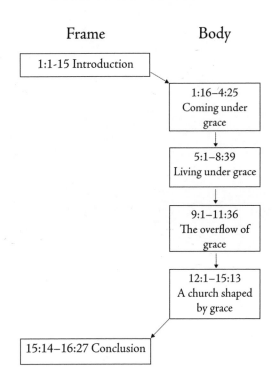

Frame

Body

1:1-15 Introduction

1:16–4:25
Coming under
grace

5:1–8:39
Living under grace

9:1–11:36
The overflow of
grace

12:1–15:13
A church shaped
by grace

15:14–16:27 Conclusion

I

Introducing Romans

Romans is a much-loved book. Parts of it are really well known. Some of the Bible's most famous texts can be found here. So, it would be easy to think that we know what Romans is all about. But do we really? Of course, in our Bibles it is neatly split up into chapters and verses and perhaps (depending on your translation) into helpful sections.

However, it's good to remember that it is a whole letter. And as such, it holds together. It's not simply a collection of well-known sayings, like a Dictionary of Quotations or a rack of postcards at the local Christian bookshop. It has a flow, a direction. It was written for a purpose.

You may think that asking questions about its meaning is unimportant. Shouldn't we just get on and read it? Yes, there's no substitute for that; however, this little book is designed to help you answer some of those questions precisely so that you can read it better. My intention is that you will be better equipped to understand Romans and apply it to twenty-first-century Christian life. Profitable Bible reading begins with careful Bible reading and that includes thinking about the letter as a whole.

My suggestion is that it is a useful exercise, before embarking on reading Romans more slowly, to read the whole letter aloud (preferably more than once), making a note of indications which tell us either about the writer and his circumstances or about the readers and

their church. This will help us get a feel
for the letter as a whole. It doesn't matter
very much exactly when Paul wrote it, or
where he wrote it from. But it matters a
great deal to know about the people to
whom he wrote it, and what was going on
with them, and therefore why he wrote it.

WHERE AND WHEN IN PAUL'S MINISTRY DID
HE WRITE ROMANS?

That said, it is not difficult to get a rough
idea of where Romans fits into Paul's
life. In 15:19-23 he says he has preached
the gospel 'from Jerusalem all the way
around to Illyricum' (roughly modern day
Albania) and that 'there is no more place for
me to work in these regions'. Presumably
he has completed the three missionary
journeys recorded in Acts, in which he has
planted churches in much of modern day
Turkey, Greece and Macedonia. He also
says (15:25) that he is about to take an aid
collection to the Christians in Jerusalem.

This is the journey recorded in Acts 20 and 21 (confirmed in Acts 24:17, where he says that this journey was 'to bring my people gifts for the poor').

It took quite a while (and significant expense) to write a letter the length of Romans. You had to employ someone actually to write what you had composed, and writing was laborious and slow. For Romans this scribe was Tertius ('who wrote down this letter' 16:22). Usually you composed a draft and then corrected it before the final version was written out, so it was not easy to do while travelling. Probably Paul wrote it during the three months he spent in Greece (Acts 20:2,3).

Most likely he was in Corinth, the capital of Achaia, a city Paul knew well. There are several hints in the letter that it was written from Corinth. In 16:1 Paul commends to them Phoebe, 'a servant of the church in Cenchreae' (the eastern port of Corinth); Phoebe may have carried the letter to Rome, since he asks them to 'receive her in the Lord' (16:2). In 16:23 he sends greetings from his host Gaius, who may be the Gaius Paul baptized in Corinth (1 Cor.1:14), and also from Erastus, 'the city's director of public works' (c.f. 2 Tim. 4:20, where Erastus 'stayed in Corinth' presumably to do his job). So Paul probably used these three months in Corinth among friends as the stable base from which to write Romans.

We are therefore to picture Paul as an experienced missionary church-planter with twenty-five years or more of pastoral experience (which is important, as we shall see). Not only has he known Jesus Christ for many years, he also knows how people 'tick' and how churches work. He has the heart and head of an experienced pastor. In particular, he understands (as every pastor ought) how doctrine is applied by preaching to change churches.

This is important for today's readers to appreciate. Paul is not the kind of old, wisened seminary professor that we might imagine. He is not a theology lecturer distanced from real life and real church. Rather, he wants his readers to know deep truths so that their lives for Christ may be transformed. Theology that has no practical impact on Christian living does not interest the Apostle, as this letter makes clear. So, we should not read Romans expecting simply to have our knowledge increased. We should expect what we read to affect our heads and our hearts, and to flow out into lives transformed by the gospel.

WHAT DO WE KNOW ABOUT THE CHURCHES IN ROME?

Paul writes (1:7) 'To all in Rome who are loved by God and called to be saints', that is, to all the Christians in Rome. Probably there was more than one assembly. Certainly there was one in the house of Priscilla and Aquila (16:5). Paul has 'planned many times to come to you' (1:13) and indeed has been longing 'for many years to see you' (15:23), so these are not brand new churches; they have a history, and this history is an important reason why he writes, as we shall see. Although Paul has not been to Rome, he knows a lot about them, as we can gather from the extraordinarily full and detailed list of greetings, the longest of all Paul's letters (16:1-16).

We know nothing about how the Christian faith came to Rome. Some Christians believe the church in Rome was founded by Peter. However, we have no firm evidence for this, or for how the gospel first reached Rome. In view of the principle of 15:20 it seems unlikely Paul would wish to 'muscle in' on churches founded by Peter, and so it seems likely that ordinary Christians such as merchants or civil servants brought the gospel to Rome on their travels.

The most important thing to know about the make-up of the churches in Rome is that they contained both Christians from a Jewish background and Christians from a Gentile background. Scholars discuss what sort of mix there might have been, and tend to think that there was probably a Gentile Christian majority. But clearly both were present. In 15:7 Paul tells them to 'accept (i.e. welcome) one another', and the context in 15:8-13 makes it clear that 'one another' here means Jewish Christians and Gentile Christians. In 2:17 he addressed the 'Jew' (presumably meaning the Christian Jew, since he is writing to Christians, 1:7). Likewise in 4:1 he calls Abraham literally 'our forefather according to the flesh', which would only be true for Jews. And in 11:13 he speaks explicitly to 'you Gentiles' (that is, Gentile Christians). As you read through the letter you will see that this mix of Jew and Gentile is enormously important (e.g. 1:16; 2:9, 10; 3:29; 9:24; 10:12).

One other fact is relevant. In Acts 18:2 Luke tells us that Paul met the Jewish Christians Aquila and Priscilla in Corinth, because the emperor 'Claudius had ordered all the Jews to leave Rome'. This may be because of civil disorder caused by the preaching of Christ, as some Roman historians have hinted. Probably Claudius expelled all the Jews, Christian and non-Christian alike (he would not have been interested in the difference) in about A.D. 49.

Claudius' edict of expulsion would have lapsed on his death in A.D. 54. Many expelled Jews presumably returned after that; there was a flourishing Jewish community in Rome under his successor Nero (A.D. 54–68). By the time Paul writes Romans (perhaps about A.D. 57) Priscilla and Aquila are back in Rome (Rom. 16:3).

We are therefore to understand a church was founded some years before as the gospel was brought to Rome by Christian merchants or civil servants. Presumably it began mostly with converts from Jewish or God-fearing backgrounds associated with the synagogue. The gospel spread to other Gentiles. Then the Jewish Christians were expelled from Rome for a few years, leaving the Gentile Christians in charge. But after Claudius' death they came back. It does not take much imagination to see the tensions this expulsion and return might have caused, and we shall return to it shortly.

THE BIG STRUCTURE OF ROMANS
(See the diagram on p. 15)

Romans begins and ends with frame sections that are very specific about the sender, the recipients, the reason for writing, and so on. This frame encloses the doctrinal and practical body of the letter. The frame begins in 1:1-15 with the greeting (1:1-7) and a word about how and why Paul is longing to preach the gospel to them (1:8-15). It ends (15:14–16:27) with Paul explaining further why he has written, what are his hopes, and a long section of personal greetings.

We may divide the body of the letter into four main parts. First, from 1:16–4:25 he expounds the gospel of justification by grace alone through faith alone (beginning with two 'manifesto' verses in 1:16, 17); I have called this 'Coming under grace'. Then in chapters 5-8 he builds on that foundation (5:1 'Therefore, since we have been justified through faith…') to teach about the Christian life, the life of the man or woman who has been justified by faith; I have called this 'Living under grace'. In chapters 9–11 he builds from the climax of chapter 8 to teach about the wise grace of God as it overflows

from Jew to Gentile and then back again
to Jew; I have called this 'The overflow of
grace'. Finally, in 12:1–15:13 he appeals
to them all by the mercies of God that
he has expounded in the letter so far, to
offer themselves as a living sacrifice, and
teaches them what this will mean in their
life as a church; I have called this 'A church
shaped by grace'.

In many ways the most important
question for any reader of Romans is how
the frame relates to the body. The frame is
very important to help us grasp why Paul
writes the letter, and therefore why he expounds
the doctrines he does in the way
he does. We shall explore this in the next
chapter.

A WORD ABOUT THE STYLE OF ROMANS
Romans is a logical letter. But it is not
linear. It is sometimes thought that Paul's
argument goes strictly from one point to
the next. But it is not as simple as that. In

particular it is worth being aware of his technique of 'trailing'. Just as a trailer will whet the appetite for an upcoming movie, so Paul will sometimes introduce a subject briefly in preparation for expanding on it later. Here are two examples:

In 6:13,19 he tells his readers to 'offer' themselves to God to be used by God. He doesn't expand on this until chapter 12, which begins with the same command to 'offer' themselves to God (12:1).

A more sustained example is the ministry of the Spirit. Chapter 8 is the great place where he speaks fully about this ministry in the believer. But he has already anticipated this ministry in 2:29, 5:5, and 7:6 (and I think implicitly also in 2:6-15).

So when reading Romans do not assume that the argument is always strictly linear; watch out for the trailers.

2

What is Romans about?

Why read Romans? You may think this is a silly question. We all know that Romans is one of the most important of all the New Testament letters (arguably the most important). So of course we need to read it. No Christian reading programme would be complete without Romans. But in fact the question is a really good one to ask.

The answer ought to be: we hope to achieve in our reading and prayerful study what Paul sought to achieve by his writing. That is, we trust that the reasons why Paul wrote Romans are the reasons why God wants us to read Romans today. There is a strong link between the two: that when God carried Paul along by his Spirit to write Romans (cf. 2 Pet. 1:21) the purpose in the mind of Paul was and is the purpose in the heart of God, and ought therefore to be the purpose in the mind and heart of the reader today.

This is a very important principle in all Bible reading and study. We need to ask not only what a Bible book or passage contains, but why it was written. For what purpose, and to what end, did the writer put pen to paper? All Bible books were written to do something. Paul did not sit down one sunny afternoon with nothing much to do and say to himself, 'I think it would be nice to jot down some edifying Christian thoughts and send them to those friendly brothers and sisters in Rome; they might be interested'.

So why does Paul write Romans? What are the reasons for Romans? Of course there are some incidental things he does, such as commend Phoebe to them (16:1f) and send lots of greetings (16:3ff). But these are extras that he takes the opportunity to do because he is writing; they are not the reason for writing.

Let us begin by considering two explanations which are inadequate, and then move to two, both of which are true and which, when held together, give us the key to the reasons for Romans. That might seem like a strange approach to take. But it's so easy to read Romans the wrong way – or at least in an inadequate way – that it is worth considering both some right and some wrong views to make sure we read Romans with the author's original intention clear in our minds.

I've introduced these views briefly now to steer us as we get into the letter. You will need to test them at every stage and in every section of the letter, to see if I have understood this aright.

TWO INADEQUATE EXPLANATIONS

1st Inadequate Explanation: Paul sets out his theology because it's a good thing to do

Romans is sometimes read as a fairly general and comprehensive exposition of Paul's gospel, written for no particular reason, except perhaps that Rome happens to be a very important city and it seems a good place to send it. It is the fruit of Paul's mature reflection on the gospel he has been preaching around the Mediterranean, the most balanced exposition of his gospel. There is some truth in this. We have seen that Paul has completed the three missionary journeys recorded in Acts; he writes with the benefit of mature reflection on his experience.

For example, his exposition of the doctrines of justification by grace alone through faith alone is more measured and nuanced than when he expounded these same truths earlier in a more desperate situation in Galatians (though neither more nor less true!). These doctrines are life-changing and central to the gospel of Christ, what Luther called 'purest gospel' and one seventeenth century Puritan 'the…perfection of saving doctrine'.

It is also true that from 1:18 through to 14:1, at least, there is little or nothing that directly and explicitly links to the situation in Rome, by contrast, for example, to the way Paul responds to issues raised in correspondence from the church in Corinth (e.g. 1 Cor. 7:1). This sustained section of the letter without explicit reference to Rome leads some to suggest that what drives Paul is the internal logic of the gospel rather than anything specific to the church in Rome and their needs; in other words, he just wants to set out his gospel.

There are several problems with this. The biggest is that it involves letting the doctrinal and ethical body of the letter float free of the enclosing frame. We will not be able to relate the frame to the body in a convincing or coherent way. Those sections will lose their meaning and purpose.

But even if the body is allowed to float free of the frame, there is still the problem that it does not read as a comprehensive or balanced exposition of Paul's gospel. Most notably, it hardly mentions the return of Jesus Christ, despite this being a very significant part of Paul's belief. The return of Christ is a core part of the gospel, and yet although Paul does mention it (in 13:11, 12), he chooses not to expand on it in this letter, because it is not the doctrine he needs to emphasize to this church at this time.

A third problem is that it is very difficult to make sense of chapters 9–11 if they are read as part of a systematic explanation of the logic of the gospel. This may be why these chapters tend to be under-emphasized in much of the church teaching we hear: how often do you hear sermons on those sections compared to the other parts of Romans?

It is true that Romans is not so obviously and tightly tied to the situation into which it is written as, say, Galatians – it is written with less urgency. But while Romans lacks the desperate intensity of Galatians, it is still written with specific purposes. It is not just what Luther's successor Melancthon called 'a compendium of Christian doctrine'.

2nd Inadequate Explanation: Paul (the apostle to the Gentiles) needs to preach to Rome (the heart of the Gentile world)

Again, there is truth in this. In 1:5 he says he has received from Jesus Christ a particular apostolic commission and grace 'for his name's sake … to call people from among all the Gentiles to the obedience that comes from faith.' And 'among all the nations' includes those in Rome (1:6). He comes back to this same 'obedience of faith' in the second last verse of the letter (16:26). In 1:9-15 he explains that he is eager to preach the gospel to them because he is eager to preach the gospel to everyone (v. 13 'the other Gentiles'). He wants to reap a harvest among them, and to encourage them by his faith, which he then expounds in the letter.

All this is true, and it moves us forward from the very general first explanation. It recognizes the significance of Rome at the heart of the Gentile world. But again it is too general. Why write this particular letter, expounding these doctrines in this way to this church at this time? And when he applies these doctrines to them in the letter, why apply them in the particular ways that he does? This explanation is still too general. While some things are worth saying to any church, Paul gives us two clear indicators of precise reasons why he wrote to this church.

Two better explanations

Paul wants the Romans to become mission partners in the gospel

In 15:14-33 Paul opens his heart to the Christians in Rome. After he has taken the collection money to Jerusalem he hopes to visit them en route for further mission in Spain. He hopes 'to have you assist me on my journey' (15:24). The verb translated 'assist … on my journey' is almost a technical term for giving practical and financial assistance. He wants them to be a missionary sending and supporting church, including prayer and material and spiritual refreshment for his ministry (15:31, 32).

In order for Rome to become a gospel-eager partnership church, they must have confidence in Paul and learn the same

passion for the gospel that he has. He tells
them he is 'eager to preach the gospel also
to you' (1:15) because he wants them to
catch this same eagerness for the gospel to
be preached to others.

So as we read Romans we need to ask,
how will this exposition of the gospel
promote a church who will be eager and
passionate to see the gospel proclaimed to
all?

*Paul wants the Romans to live in harmony
with one another*
Throughout the letter we see indications
that Paul is very concerned about harmony between Jews and Gentiles in the
church. We see this almost whenever
he applies his doctrines. For example
in 3:27 his conclusion from the doctrine
of justification by grace is the exclusion
of boasting, because boasting disrupts
harmony. In chapter 12 he is concerned to
see the Christian body working together

in harmony (e.g. vv. 3-8, 10, 16). In 14:1–
15:13 the 'strong' and the 'weak' reflect
Jew/Gentile distinctions and his aim is
that they should accept and welcome one
another as Christ has welcomed them
(15:7).

He wants them to pray for his journey
taking a collection from Gentile churches
to Jewish Christians in Jerusalem (15:22-
33) and they will only do this if they
understand deeply how the gospel unites
Jew and Gentile in Christ. The Jew/
Gentile issue runs right through the letter.
Indeed over 60 per cent of all Paul's uses
of the word 'law' (generally referring to
the Law of Moses) occur in Romans (74
out of 121).

The social background of Claudius' expulsion of the Jews and their subsequent
return makes perfect sense of all this.
Probably the first senior members of the
church in Rome were Jewish Christians.
This is likely because they would have

heard the gospel first ('first for the Jew' 1:16), they would have known the Scriptures better, and when the light dawned on them that Jesus of Nazareth was the Messiah, the Christ, all the pieces of the jigsaw would have fallen into place (as they did with Paul at his conversion).

But for the Gentiles, the pieces of the jigsaw were not even there in the first place; they had to be taught the Scriptures and what the word 'Christ' means. So, to start with, we may imagine Jews with names like Joseph, the church secretary, and Simeon, the church treasurer, sharing a quiet pleasure in their positions as the obvious ones to run the church. Of course, with their privileged background, they were the natural ones to choose. And then disaster strikes – Claudius expels them. Someone has to take over – Gentiles with names like Linus and Julius fill their positions.

Then the emperor Claudius dies; and Joseph and Simeon and the other Jewish Christians return, and perhaps expect to be reinstated to their positions of influence. Perhaps Linus and Julius have different ideas. The church in Rome would not naturally be a place of harmony and peace. Only the gospel of justification by grace could make it so.

So Paul expounds the gospel in Romans with the aim of bringing Jew and Gentile together in harmony in the church. And so as we read Romans we need to ask, how will this exposition of the gospel promote a church today who live together in love? Look out for these issues as you read the letter.

Although I think both these precise reasons run like threads through Romans, I think we may see a stronger emphasis on mission in the frame of the letter, both in 1:1-15 and then in 15:14-33. And there is generally a stronger emphasis on the unity of the Jews and Gentiles in the church in the doctrinal body of the letter. This leads us to ask how the two precise reasons are connected.

Putting the precise reasons together: the key to reading Romans

These two precise reasons immediately make Romans of great importance for every Christian. Most of the difficulties in churches concern unity and/or mission. Sometimes it is an issue concerning the unity and harmony of the local church fellowship; sometimes it concerns the unity of a small group or even a leadership team.

At other times, godly Christians are only too aware that the church to which they belong is an inward-looking fellowship and they long to know how it might be turned outwards to the needy world, not simply for growth (for every human society is concerned with survival), but for crossing barriers into other people groups, other cultures, reaching unlikely people with the barrier-breaking message of Christ. We are bound to be concerned with this, unless that is, we are happy to have 'Jews' and 'Gentiles' enjoying happily mono-cultural and separate churches.

But although these two concerns are high on any church's priority list, on the face of it they are different and separate. One is to do with evangelism and mission, looking outwards with zeal. The other is to do with unity and harmony, looking inwards to build a new society in the church. One is about eagerness, the other about harmony; one about partnership, the other about peace.

In fact the connection is profound, and could only be made by an apostle shaped by knowing the risen Lord through years of practical sharp-end Christian church-planting and pastoral ministry. Paul understands that the full gospel, which is the foundation of justification (chs. 1–4), the ministry of the Spirit in the life of

the believer (chs. 5–8), and the wise sov-
ereignty of God in conversion (chs. 9–11)
is the key both to gospel partnership and
to church harmony. Only a church deeply
soaked in the gospel will live in harmony;
only a church thoroughly taught the gospel will reach out with zeal.

The reason is that only the gospel
humbles men and women to the level of
the ground, so that human pride ceases
to make divisions and the church ceases
to be a club, but reaches out (from floor
level, as it were) to fellow sinners in love.
A 'church' that is not shaped by the gospel
may well reach out to others. Of course
it will be concerned with growth, as any
society will be that is concerned with its
survival. But the outreach will inevitably
be focused on 'people like us' (whoever
we may be). Only the gospel enables us to
live together with people unlike us and to
reach out across human barriers to people
very different from us.

Every human society or community is by nature both inward-looking and unstable. It is inward-looking, because it is always more comfortable to be a club to which only 'people like us' belong. And it is unstable, because I in my pride will always want to be narrowing the definition of 'people like us', so that it becomes 'people like me'. Human pride leads to human strife which divides a society from within; and human pride leads to dividing walls of hostility which cut us off from the world outside. The gospel therefore needs to counteract both internal instability and external defensiveness. And it does both in exactly the same way, by humbling human pride.

There is no such thing as a church that just exists for evangelism, or a church that just focuses on building itself up in love. For only a church that lives in harmony under Christ can reach out effectively with zeal. Unless its members understand their status under grace, they will be riven with rivalries and party spirit, always at one another's throats or biting behind one another's backs. And evangelism will disappear off the agenda.

And the same is true the other way around. For only a church that reaches out with zeal can live in harmony. When a church ceases to reach out, they become practical unbelievers in the gospel of grace; and when they become practical unbelievers in grace reaching out, they become practical unbelievers in grace bringing harmony within. If I don't really believe that the offer of grace is for all outside the church, then I will not believe that it is for all inside the church. And as soon as I forget that, my relations within the church become marked by non-acceptance of those who are not like me. And so my lack of evangelistic zeal bounces back into divisions within the church.

As we read Romans, therefore, keep on asking how this particular teaching of the gospel impacts these two precise aims of the letter: evangelistic zeal and church harmony. I hope you will see that the reasons why Paul writes the letter dovetail with the gospel as he expounds it in the letter. The logic of the gospel as Paul expounds it will press us, like them, out into the world, and at the same time build us up together in love.

To anticipate the argument of the letter, let me state in simple terms the doctrinal key both to unity and mission. **It is to lift Jesus very high and bring you and me very low**, or – to put it in more theological language – it is to magnify grace (which lifts Jesus high) and to emphasize faith (which brings me low, since it speaks of coming empty-handed to the Cross, 'nothing in my hand I bring…'). It is this Jesus-exalting, people-humbling gospel that Paul expounds in Romans.

We may set these two tightly-linked purposes into the bigger framework of the glory of God. Paul's great aim in Romans is that God should be glorified, and in particular that the glory of his grace should be visible in the supernatural phenomenon of a united and missionary church. We may therefore say that

the purpose of Romans

is the glory of God

seen in a united missionary church

humbled together under grace.

3

The everyone gospel

Think of the most non-Christian person you know, perhaps an ardent advocate of another religion, maybe an aggressive atheist, or an out and out seeker of pleasure. Now think of the most consistently Christian person you know, someone of integrity, zeal, Christlike maturity and spiritual giftedness. What do these two have in common, apart from a shared humanity? Paul begins his letter with the answer to this question, that both are sinners in desperate need of the gospel of the Lord Jesus. It is an answer that is crucial to the health of the church and the blessing of the world. Verses 1-15 are the opening part of the 'frame' of the letter, which lead straight in to verses 16 and 17, the 'manifesto' which headlines the first doctrinal section.

THE GREETING (1:1-7): THE EVERYONE GOSPEL

Paul's readers would have been astonished by the theologically meaty way in which he introduces himself. Verses 1-6 are by far the longest of all Paul's introductions, not because he needs to tell them a lot about himself, but because he wants to introduce his gospel.

> 1:1Paul,
> a servant of Christ Jesus,
> called to be an apostle
> and set apart for the gospel of God —

His focus here (unlike Galatians, for example) is not on his authority, but on his commission, to be 'an apostle…set apart for the gospel of God'. Paul uses the words 'gospel' or 'preach the gospel' twelve times in Romans (1:1, 9, 15, 16; 2:16; 10:15, 16; 11:28; 15:16, 19, 20; 16:25). Seven of these are in his frame, showing how important the gospel is to this letter. Paul wants to tell them about his gospel more than he wants to tell them about himself. It is as if he begins by saying, 'The only reason I want you to listen to me is because I want you to grasp the gospel of the Lord Jesus Christ.' So, while this is a greeting in its shape, it is Paul's headline teaching point in its substance.

²the gospel he promised beforehand through his prophets in the Holy Scriptures

This is the gospel God 'promised beforehand through his prophets in the Holy Scriptures'. Here the 'prophets' are shorthand for all the Old Testament authors, including, for example, Moses (Deut. 34:10) and David (Acts 2:30). This short statement is full of meaning for every Christian.

The gospel cannot be understood from the New Testament alone, but needs the Old Testament as well (you will find that the Old Testament is quoted a lot in Romans; most Bible translations reflect this in the footnotes).

The Old Testament is only understood as fulfilled in Jesus Christ. Christ does not change the meaning of the Old Testament; rather he is the key to understanding what the Old Testament really means.

The Old Testament is fundamentally about the promise that 'Abraham and his offspring...would be heir of the world' (4:13, Paul's summary of Gen. 12:1-3; 15:5; 17:5,6 etc.). The gospel is God doing what he had promised to do, giving the government of the world to Abraham's offspring. When Paul speaks of 'the gospel…promised beforehand' he is not speaking of a random collection of predictions dotted through the Old Testament; he speaks of one coherent promise attested by the whole of the Old Testament.

> [3]the gospel…regarding his Son, who as to his human nature was a descendant of David,
>
> [4]and who through the Spirit of holiness was declared with power to be the Son of God [was appointed the Son of God in power] by his resurrection from the dead:
> Jesus Christ our Lord.

The fulfilment of promise leads in to verses 3 and 4, the heart of Paul's introduction. Notice how Jesus Christ both begins and ends these verses. The gospel is 'regarding his Son… Jesus Christ our Lord.' Paul teaches four truths about Jesus:

1. He is God's Son, like Israel, corporately (Exod. 4:22, 'Israel is my firstborn son'), and the Davidic kings, representatively (2 Sam. 7:14, 'I will be his father, and he shall be my son').

2. Therefore it is no surprise that Jesus was 'as to his human nature… a descendant of David', the heir to David's throne.

3. The resurrection changed the state of Jesus. The literal meaning of verse 4 is that Jesus 'was appointed the Son of God in power by his resurrection from the dead'. The word translated 'appointed' means something like 'crowned'. It is not just that the resurrection publicly showed us who Jesus had always been (NIV 'declared'); rather, at the resurrection the one who had always been Son of God was changed

from being 'the Son of God in weakness' to being 'the Son of God in power'. The Holy Spirit, who is the executive arm of the Godhead on earth, raised him from a body of weakness to a resurrection body of power (c.f. Phil. 2:6-11). The resurrection has been called the turning point in the existence of the Son of God.

4. Consequently he is not only 'Jesus' (the man), but also 'Christ' (Messiah, anointed King), 'our Lord' (the ruler of all and heir of the world).

…Jesus Christ our Lord,

[5]through whom we received grace and apostleship to the obedience of faith
among all the Gentiles
for the sake of his name,

[6]among whom are you also
who are called of Jesus Christ.[1]

---

1   Author's translation

It is helpful to have verses 5 and 6 in a more literal translation and order than the NIV. Paul explains what the resurrection means for his job as an apostle. 'Jesus Christ our Lord' is the powerful agent 'through whom we' (Paul and his fellow apostles) 'have received grace and apostleship' (which means grace to do his job as an apostle). But what is the job of an apostle? Paul tells us the goal and scope of his apostleship and the deepest reason for it.

The goal of apostleship: the obedience of faith
His apostleship is 'to' (which means, 'aiming for') 'the obedience of faith.' Paul uses this important phrase right at the start here, and also in the second last verse of the letter (lit. 'to bring all nations to the obedience of faith' 16:26). What does this mean? 'The obedience of faith' means bowing the knee in trusting submission to Jesus the Lord, both at the start and all through the Christian life.

One common understanding of 'the obedience of faith' is that 'faith' is the main thing, and obedience is the consequence of faith; first we believe, and then we obey (NIV 'the obedience that comes from faith' 1:5). True faith always results in obedience, but faith and obedience are distinct. This gives the impression that 'faith' is primary and 'obedience' secondary, a consequence of faith (albeit a necessary consequence).

If this were so, we would expect that when Paul abbreviates the expression, he would always abbreviate it to 'faith' (if this is the primary meaning). In fact, he is quite likely to abbreviate it to 'obedience'. So, for example, he can rejoice that their 'faith is being reported all over the world' (1:8) and equally that 'Everyone has heard about your obedience' (16:19). He describes his ministry as bringing the Gentiles 'to obedience' (15:18), where we might have expected him to speak of bringing them to faith.

It is important to be clear that the basis on which we are justified before God is not our obedience. We find in Romans 5 that, just as the disobedience of Adam made us all sinners, so we are made righteous not by our obedience but 'by the obedience of the one man', Jesus Christ (5:19). Theologians sometimes speak of Jesus' active obedience in his human life, obeying his Father every moment of the day and night (the actions of his life), and his 'passive' obedience on the cross, when he obeyed by submitting to suffering (his passion at the end of his life).

Together, Jesus' life and death form one great act of obedience. It is through his obedience that we are justified. We are not justified by anything we have done, can do, or ever will do, but entirely by what Jesus did for us. But having established the basis of our justification entirely in God's grace through Jesus, we still need to clarify the nature of saving faith. What does it mean to exercise saving faith in Jesus?

First, our initial repentance and faith is obedience to the command of God. In the gospel, God 'commands all people everywhere to repent' (Acts 17:30). To repent is therefore to obey God's command at the start of the Christian life. This is why the New Testament speaks of unbelievers as those who 'do not obey the gospel' (2 Thess. 1:8; Rom. 10:16 - where NIV 'accepted' is literally 'obeyed'). To believe is to obey the teaching of grace (6:17). We do not believe and then obey; we obey by believing. We give up trying to establish our own righteous status before God and surrender to his (9:31, 32; 10:3).

Second, ongoing faith means ongoing obedience. We do not obey at the start and then just content ourselves with believing after that. The Christian life consists of ongoing disobedience to sin's demands (6:12) and ongoing obedience to God (6:16), a glad slavery to righteousness (6:18). This obedience is expressed by practical submission to Christ's apostles and their teaching (2 Thess. 3:14; Phil. 2:12). Ongoing obedience is the outworking of our salvation (Phil. 2:12); it is not a subsequent thing, a consequence of faith; it is faith in its concrete expression. This is why James says: 'As the body without the spirit is dead, so faith without works is dead' (James 2:26). Our works (our actual obedience) are the life-giving breath that breathes life into what will otherwise be a dead 'faith' (that is, not a real faith at all).

Let us come back to my definition: 'The obedience of faith' means bowing the knee in trusting submission to Jesus the Lord, both at the start and all through the Christian life. The words 'trusting submission' capture the nature and the benefits of faith. The nature of faith is submission, bowing the knee to the King. The benefits of faith are the benefits of coming under the gracious rule of this King, which is why this submission is a trusting submission. When we bow the knee to King Jesus, we entrust ourselves to his rule, trusting that under his lordship we will experience the blessings of his saving righteousness. We cannot come under his gracious protection without coming under his rule; there is no salvation without submission. We benefit from his rescue not just by believing that it is true, but by submitting to him.

The obedience of faith is therefore a trusting submission to Jesus the Lord, bowing the knee to him at the start (initial faith) and going on bowing the knee to him thereafter (continuing faith). The obedience of faith is an initial and an ongoing surrender.

'The obedience of faith' helps us rightly to understand both obedience and faith, which are two ways of speaking of the same thing. Authentic faith is both a receiving and a surrender, and it is followed by ongoing receiving and ongoing surrender. True faith in Christ consists in bowing the knee in trusting submission to him as Lord. This obedience is the goal of Paul's apostleship.

The scope of apostleship: the whole world
Paul also tells us the scope of his apostleship, which is 'among all the Gentiles.' Because Jesus has been crowned King over all and heir of the promise to Abraham to inherit the world (4:13), it follows that the whole world is summoned to trusting submission to him. The gospel is 'the everyone gospel' because Jesus is 'the everyone Lord'. And therefore 'you also' (v. 6) are included. There is nothing special about Rome, however important they may think they are. Rome is just one more place where men and women are summoned to bow the knee to Jesus the Lord.

The deepest reason for apostleship: the glory of Jesus

Apostleship is 'for the sake of (Jesus') name'. When men and women bow the knee to him, the honour goes to Jesus alone. They are Christians not fundamentally because they decided to be (though they did), but because they are 'called of Jesus Christ' (v. 6), which probably means not just 'called to belong to Jesus Christ' (NIV) but also 'called by Jesus Christ', since the usual meaning of 'call' in Romans is the sovereign call of God (e.g. 8:30).

> ⁷To all in Rome who are loved by God and called to be saints:
>
> Grace and peace to you from God our Father and from the Lord Jesus Christ.

He writes to 'all in Rome who are loved by God and called to be saints' (i.e. Christians, set apart by and for God). The love starts with God, the call comes from God, and the honour goes to God. He greets 'all' of them because he is concerned for their harmony.

It is on the basis of this great fact, the 'everyone gospel', that Paul goes on to speak of the kind of relationship he has with his readers.

RELATIONSHIP (1:8-15): THE EAGER PREACHER

[8]First, I thank my God through Jesus Christ for all of you, because your faith is being reported all over the world. [9]God, whom I serve with my whole heart in preaching the gospel of his Son, is my witness how constantly I remember you [10]in my prayers at all times; and I pray that now at last by God's will the way may be opened for me to come to you.

[11]I long to see you so that I may impart to you some spiritual gift [grace gift] to make you strong— [12]that is, that you and I may be mutually encouraged by each other's faith. [13]I do not want you

to be unaware, brothers, that I planned many times to come to you (but have been prevented from doing so until now) in order that I might have a harvest [fruit] among you, just as I have had among the other Gentiles.

Just as Paul turned a conventional greeting into his first teaching point in verses 1-7, so now in verses 8-15 he turns a conventional expression of relationship into an opportunity to develop this teaching point.

The tone changes from the proclamation of fact in verses 1-6, to the expression of eager longing in verses 8-15. This section is full of verbs expressing emotion and desire. He thanks God, serves God wholeheartedly, prays constantly, longs to see them, and has planned many times to come and see them. Above all, he is 'eager to preach the gospel' to these Christians in Rome. The key to this passage is to see how the fact proclaimed in verses 1-7 leads to the eagerness of verses 8-15.

The theme of 'all' continues. He has spoken of 'all the Gentiles' (v. 5), 'you also' (v. 6), 'all in Rome' (v. 7); now he continues with 'all of you… all over the world' (v. 8), 'Greeks and barbarians… wise and foolish' (v. 14), and 'also to you' (v. 15). All sorts of people have submitted, in the obedience of faith, to the 'everyone Lord' through the preaching of the 'everyone gospel'. Many more will do the same.

Notice also the emphasis on faith. Paul thanks God 'because your faith is being reported all over the world' (v. 8). The sharing of faith leads to harmony and mutual encouragement, whereas boasting of works divides. When we speak of our works we puff ourselves up, we want people to give glory to us, for our initiative, achievement or virtue. This always leads to strife, as everyone knows from the school playground onwards. But

when we speak of our faith, we proclaim
the goodness of Jesus. Our faith is the
conclusive proof that we contribute
nothing and God does everything. The
'harvest [fruit]' Paul longs for is the work
of God in changing lives to righteousness
(as in Isa. 5:1-7), both by new conversions
and by growth in godliness.

> [14]I am bound [under obligation]
> both to Greeks and non-Greeks [bar-
> barians],
> both to the wise and the foolish.
>
> [15]That is why I am so eager to preach
> the gospel also to you who are at Rome.

In verse 14 he draws the logical step from
'the everyone Lord' and 'the everyone
gospel' to the eager preacher. He is
'under obligation both to Greeks' (that is,
educated people who speak Greek, just as
educated people in medieval Europe would
have spoken Latin) 'and barbarians' (an

insulting onomatopoeic word, uneducated dimwits, who speak gobbledegook!). (Paul uses the same word 'barbarians' in 1 Cor. 14:11 of unintelligible speech.) He owes the gospel 'both to the wise' (that is, those who consider themselves clever, Greek-speakers) 'and the foolish' (that is, those considered stupid by clever people). The 'Greek' is put right with God in exactly the same way as the 'barbarian' (cf. 1 Cor. 1:18–2:5). Each of them comes empty-handed (that is, with faith) or they do not come at all.

Why is Paul 'under obligation'? The metaphor of a monetary debt doesn't capture the urgency. It is like a city being conquered by a new king, who entrusts to the herald the proclamation of his victory and the offer of his pardon. The herald therefore owes it to all the citizens to tell them urgently. If he does not, they will incur the anger of the new king by not bowing the knee to him and accepting his pardon.

This urgency makes Paul 'eager to preach the gospel also to you who are at Rome' (v. 15).

REASON (1:16, 17): THE RIGHTEOUSNESS OF GOD
Paul now leads straight in to the headline manifesto which sets the agenda to the end of chapter 4.

> ¹⁶For I am not ashamed of the gospel,
>
> because it is the power of God for the salvation of everyone who believes:
>> first for the Jew, then for the Gentile [Greek].
>
> ¹⁷For in the gospel a righteousness from God [the righteousness of God] is revealed,
>
>> a righteousness that is by faith from first to last [from faith to faith], just as it is written: 'The righteous will live by faith.' (Hab. 2:4)

Notice the three connecting words ('For… because…For…', all the same word in Greek).

Why am I eager to preach the gospel to you (v. 15)? Because I am not ashamed of the gospel. He is eager because he is not ashamed (cf. 2 Tim. 1:8). The fear of shame will make us less than eager to preach the gospel, even if we know we ought to do it ('under obligation' v. 14). To be 'ashamed' includes having a subjective sense of shame (feeling ashamed). But the main Bible meaning is objective: to be ashamed is to be publicly disgraced, to be shown to be in the wrong. No doubt Paul sometimes feels the weakness of the gospel in the eyes of the world (cf. 1 Cor. 1:18). But he is confident that in the last day he will not be held up to shame as one who has preached something untrue and ineffective.

Why am I not ashamed of the gospel? Because it is the power of God to rescue. He is not ashamed because the gospel is not weak (though it may seem so). Every human being God rescues, he will rescue by the gospel of Jesus. No one anywhere or at any time (including before Christ) will have been rescued in any other way. Paul will devote 1:18–3:20 to proving this controversial assertion.

'Salvation' refers not to becoming a Christian, but to the final rescue at the end of the Christian life. Christians have already been justified, but will not be fully saved until the end (5:9, 10). 'Salvation is nearer to us now than when we first believed' (13:11). The gospel is God's instrument not only to make us Christian in the first place, but also to keep us Christian to the end. This is another reason why he is eager to preach the gospel to the Christians.

The emphasis is that it is God's power to rescue 'everyone who believes…first… the Jew, then…the Gentile.' This continues the theme of 'all' or 'everyone' we have seen in verses 1-15. Paul again uses the expression 'everyone who believes' in 3:22; 4:11

and 10:4 (and cf. 10:11). In the missionary journeys in Acts they went 'first to the
Jew'. But the gospel that saves the Jew is the
same gospel as that which saves the Gentile. Neither contributes anything of their
own, except the sin from which they need to
be rescued. We do not even contribute our
faith, for faith itself is a gift from God.

But the big question is this: why is
the gospel God's power to rescue all who
believe? This is the climax of the manifesto:
'For in the gospel the righteousness of
God is revealed, a righteousness that is
by faith from first to last [from faith to
faith], just as it is written: "The righteous
will live by faith"'(Hab. 2:4).

Let us unpack the four parts of
verse 17. What is 'the righteousness of
God'? What does it mean for it to be 'revealed' in the gospel? Why is it 'from faith
to faith'? How does the Old Testament
quotation help us understand it?

What is 'the righteousness of God'?
This important expression is used eight times in Romans (1:17; 3:5, 21, 22, 25, 26; 10:3a, 3b) and once elsewhere in Paul's letters (2 Cor. 5:21). It covers three important elements: who God is, what he does, and how he does it.

- It is an attribute of God's character, 'God's righteousness' (something that belongs to him). In himself, he is just, true, utterly fair, consistent, glorious and holy. His 'righteousness' is the utter rightness of his character, right to the core of his glorious being.

- It is an activity of God's person, 'the righteousness shown by God' (something he does), not a static quality but a dynamic activity, God 'doing the right thing,' especially by keeping his promises. Righteousness is God reaching out to rescue people, as he said he would do. It is therefore an expression of his power to save (as here in v. 16). We see this meaning clearly in the Old Testament, for example, in Psalm 98:2, 3a, where his 'salvation', his 'righteousness', his 'love' (that is, covenant steadfast love), and his 'faithfulness' (that is, to his promises), all stand in parallel and mean much the same thing (cf. 1 Sam. 12:7 where Samuel speaks literally of 'the righteousness of the LORD for you and your fathers'). God's righteousness is his saving activity.

• It is a free gift of God to the believer, a status of right relationship with God freely conferred by grace, 'a righteousness from God' (something that God gives to us, as conveyed in NIV). This meaning is explicit in

Philippians 3:9 where it is literally 'a righteousness from God.' This status is a legal (forensic) declaration. It concerns an instantaneous change in status before God and not inner moral transformation (for which we must wait until later in the letter).

In summary, we may take 'the righteousness of God' to mean his activity in reaching out to rescue all who trust in Christ by giving them, as an undeserved gift, a right status before him. In other words, it is the doctrine of justification by grace alone received by faith alone.

What does it mean for the righteousness of God to be 'revealed' in the gospel?
God did not begin rescuing people after Jesus came. He began with Adam's son Abel (Heb. 11:4). Whenever he rescued anyone, he did it 100 per cent by grace, and they received it 100 per cent by faith (and 0 per cent by their own merit). What the gospel did was to

show clearly why and how he does it. A useful analogy (attributed to Augustine) is that the Old Testament is like a fully-furnished but darkened room. All the 'furniture' of God's rescue is present, but it is only perceived dimly and in shadow. The gospel turns the light on so that we say, 'Ah, now I can see what God has been doing and how he has been doing it!' You will see this more clearly when you get to 3:21-26. In the gospel the righteousness of God 'is being revealed', a present continuous tense, meaning an ongoing activity. Everywhere the gospel is preached, a light is shone on God's rescue work.

Why is the righteousness of God 'from faith to faith'?

This expression seems to be an emphatic way of saying that the righteousness of God is only appropriated by those who come empty-handed (which is what faith means) and rely 100 per cent on his grace. Justification (the legal declaration of righteousness) is given by grace alone and received by faith alone.

How does the Old Testament quotation help us understand the righteousness of God?
Paul quotes from Habakkuk 2:4 (quoted also in Gal. 3:11 and Heb. 10:38). It is worth looking up in its context, since the New Testament writers never make a text that meant one thing mean something contradictory. They bring out the full meaning that the Old Testament text originally had. In Habakkuk 2 the believer waits for the appointed time when God's promises will be fulfilled. Fulfilment seems slow, but it will come (Hab. 2:3); what God has promised, he will do.

There are two possible responses, then as now. Some will be 'puffed up' (v. 4a) with a proud self-sufficiency that thinks it can cope on its own. By contrast, 'the righteous' (that is, those who believe the promises) 'will live by his faith.' His believing the promise will both bring him into right relation with God (the main emphasis in Romans), and also keep him in right relation (the emphasis in Heb. 10:38). So faith is taking God at his word. The opposite of faith is pride. Either I wait for God to rescue me, or I think I can rescue myself.

APPLYING THIS PASSAGE TO OURSELVES

In this short introductory section, there is much for a Christian reader to take in and pray through. In particular, we need to grasp that:

- the gospel centres on a person. It is not an '-ism' and it is not do's and don'ts.

- the Old Testament explains Jesus. To say that we can understand Christianity without the Old Testament is to miss the way Paul says Jesus fulfils the Bible story.

- the resurrection crowns Jesus the Lord of all human beings without exception: not just certain races, not just clever or educated people, not just people in some countries. Think about unlikely people in our families, workplaces, neighbourhoods, people of other religions, atheists. He is Lord of them all. Engage with the harmful challenge of the pluralist agendas that would confine Jesus to the private sphere of 'values' rather than the public realm of 'facts'.

- 'faith' does not simply mean 'believing something to be true' but is shorthand for 'the obedience of faith' which means trusting submission to Jesus.

- we should long for the name of Jesus to be honoured as all kinds of people all over the world bow the knee to him.

- the sharing of our faith (rather than boasting about our works) encourages and unites, and apply this to our conversations: how much are we talking about ourselves, and how much are we singing and speaking the praises of Jesus?

- Paul's words address the most common reasons why we may be ashamed of the gospel, namely:

  - we fear it isn't true. The resurrection proves that it is true.
  - we worry it isn't relevant to some people. The resurrection proves it is relevant for everybody.
  - we are not sure it is powerful, because it seems such a weak and pathetic message. And yet it is the way God has chosen to save those he saves.

- there is an obligation to take the gospel to every human being. If we do not seek to do this, we are treating people as if they were sub-human (since we are not under obligation to preach the gospel to cats and dogs).

- we ought to be eager for gospel partnership:
  - in prayer for non-Christians and for other gospel workers.
  - in our own courageous testimony to Jesus.
  - in working together in evangelism, helping one another build friendships with non-Christians and share the gospel of Jesus with them.
  - in financial partnership with those needing support in gospel work.
  - for some, who have the gifts, being equipped and supported for public preaching.

- in practical support for gospel work, e.g. cooking for an enquirers' course.

- in inviting non-Christians to events where they will hear the gospel of Jesus.

- Christianity is a rescue religion. It is about salvation, not about becoming more knowledgeable, respectable, secure or feeling good about ourselves.

- we Christians ought never to tire of hearing the gospel and all that it implies!

Questions for personal or group study

Why not use some of these questions as a personal study on the passage? Alternatively, sit down with a friend or a small group to look at Romans 1:1-17 together and work through the text using these questions. Remember to pray in the lessons you learn.

To clarify understanding
1. What did God promise in the Old Testament (v. 2) and how do verses 3 and 4 clarify this (cf. 4:13)?

2. What did the resurrection do for Jesus
    (v. 4)? (i.e. What is the significance of
    the resurrection, what does the resur-
    rection mean?)

3. What was the aim of Paul's job as an
    apostle (v. 5)?

4. For what reasons does Paul want to
    visit the church in Rome (vv. 8-15)?

5. Why is Paul not ashamed of the gos-
    pel (v. 16)?

6. Why is the gospel God's power to res-
    cue anybody who believes (v. 17)?

To encourage honest response

1. Why is it hard to say that Jesus is King
    of all the world, in the workplace,
    school, neighbourhood, etc? What are
    we worried about, if we say this?

2. How do verses 1-7 help us to do this?
    (i.e. In what ways do the truths of

these verses help us engage honestly
with pluralist friends?)

3. Why is it encouraging to see lives
changed by faith, in people who are
different from us? How can we promote
this kind of mutual encouragement in
our church, in mission partnerships, etc?

4. How can we be a church that works
together in gospel eagerness in our
neighbourhood?

5. How does the truth of verses 16 and
17 promote harmony between different kinds of people in our church fellowship?

Editor's Note

If you have found this little volume useful you might like to consider the two volumes written by Christopher in our *Teaching...* series. They are designed for preachers and Bible study leaders and will take you through the text of Romans in a similar way to the way we've tackled Romans 1:1-17 above. They also contain help to think through how each passage might be preached or taught and how a Bible study or sermon series may be put together.

Introducing Series

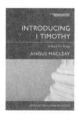

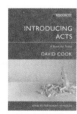

978-1-78191-060-3

978-1-84550-824-1

978-1-78191-059-7

978-1-78191-158-7

978-1-78191-233-1

These are books which will equip you for your own study of Ephesians, 1 Timothy, Acts, Numbers, Daniel and Romans, ultimately in teaching them. It will help you answer the questions: Why did things happen the way they did? Why should we read these books of the Bible today? What are the main themes? These are Pocket Guide versions of *Teaching 1 Timothy* (978-1-84550-808-1), *Teaching Acts* (978-1-84550-255-3), *Teaching Ephesians* (978-1-84550-684-1), *Teaching Numbers* (978-1-78191-156-3), *Teaching Romans vol. 1* (978-1-84550-455-7) and *Teaching Romans vol. 2* (978-1-84550-456-4). Each includes an introductory study.

Christopher Ash is Director of the Cornhill Training Course, a one-year course designed to provide Bible-handling and practical ministry skills to those exploring their future role in Christian work, and an active member of Christ Church Mayfair in central London.

Simon Austen has degrees in Science and Theology. A previous chaplain of Stowe School in Buckinghamshire, he is now Vicar of Houghton and Kingmoor in Carlisle, England.

David Cook has recently retired from his role as Principal and Director of the School of Preaching at Sydney Missionary and Bible College (SMBC). He is now involved in an itinerant preaching and teaching ministry.

Angus MacLeay is the Rector of St Nicholas, a large Anglican church in Sevenoaks, Kent, and is also a member of the Church of England General Synod.

Adrian Reynolds is Director of Ministry of The Proclamation Trust and also serves as associate minister at East London Tabernacle Baptist Church.

PT Resources

www.proctrust.org.uk
Resources for preachers and Bible teachers

PT Resources, a ministry of The Proclamation Trust, provides a range of multimedia resources for preachers and Bible teachers.

Books

The *Teaching the Bible* series, published jointly with *Christian Focus Publications*, is written by preachers, for preachers, and is specifically geared to the purpose of God's Word – its proclamation as living truth. Books in the series aim to help the reader move beyond simply understanding a text to communicating and applying it.

Current titles include: *Teaching 1 Peter, Teaching 1 Timothy, Teaching Acts, Teaching Amos, Teaching Ephesians, Teaching Isaiah, Teaching Matthew, Teaching Numbers, Teaching Romans,* and *Teaching the Christian Hope.*

Forthcoming titles include: *Teaching Daniel, Teaching 1 and 2 Kings,* and *Teaching Nehemiah.*

DVD TRAINING

Preaching & Teaching the Old Testament:
4 DVDs – Narrative, Prophecy, Poetry, Wisdom

Preaching & Teaching the New Testament
3 DVDs – Gospels, Letters, Acts & Revelation

These training DVDs aim to give preachers and teachers confidence in handling the rich variety of God's Word. David Jackman has taught this material to generations of Cornhill students, and gives us step-by-step instructions on handling each genre of biblical literature.

He demonstrates principles that will guide us through the challenges of teaching and applying different parts of the Bible, for example:

- How does prophecy relate to the lives of its hearers – ancient and modern?
- How can you preach in a way that reflects the deep emotion of the Psalms?

Both sets are suitable for preachers and for those teaching the Bible in a wide variety of contexts.

- Designed for **individual** and **group** study
- Interactive learning through many **worked examples** and **exercises**
- Flexible format ideal for **training courses**
- Optional **English subtitles** for second-language users
- Print as many **workbooks** as you need (PDF)

Audio
PT Resources has a large range of Mp3 downloads, nearly all of which are entirely free to download and use.

Preaching Instruction
This series aims to help the preacher or teacher understand, open up and teach individual books of the Bible by getting to grips with their central message and purpose.

Sermon Series
These sermons, examples of great preaching, not only demonstrate faithful biblical preaching but will also refresh and instruct the hearer.

Conferences
Recordings of our conferences include challenging topical addresses, discussion of preaching and ministry issues, and warm-hearted exposition that will challenge and inspire all those in ministry.

Christian Focus Publications

Our mission statement –

STAYING FAITHFUL
In dependence upon God we seek to impact the world through literature faithful to His infallible Word, the Bible. Our aim is to ensure that the Lord Jesus Christ is presented as the only hope to obtain forgiveness of sin, live a useful life and look forward to heaven with Him.

Our books are published in four imprints:

CHRISTIAN
FOCUS

popular works including biographies, commentaries, basic doctrine and Christian living.

CHRISTIAN
HERITAGE

books representing some of the best material from the rich heritage of the church.

MENTOR

books written at a level suitable for Bible College and seminary students, pastors, and other serious readers. The imprint includes commentaries, doctrinal studies, examination of current issues and church history.

CF4•K

children's books for quality Bible teaching and for all age groups: Sunday school curriculum, puzzle and activity books; personal and family devotional titles, biographies and inspirational stories – Because you are never too young to know Jesus!

Christian Focus Publications Ltd,
Geanies House, Fearn, Ross-shire,
IV20 1TW, Scotland, United Kingdom.
www.christianfocus.com